How to Write a Letter

by Cecilia Minden
and Kate Roth

CHERRY LAKE PUBLISHING · ANN ARBOR, MICHIGAN

CHERRY LAKE
Publishing

Published in the United States of America by Cherry Lake Publishing
Ann Arbor, Michigan
www.cherrylakepublishing.com

Content Adviser: Jeannette Mancilla-Martinez, EdD, Assistant Professor of
Literacy, Language, and Culture, University of Illinois at Chicago

Design and Illustration: The Design Lab

Photo Credits: Page 4, ©iStockphoto.com/ktaylorg; page 6, ©Tatiana
Popova/Shutterstock, Inc.; page 10, ©vblinov/Shutterstock, Inc.; page 11,
©Jeffrey Moore/Shutterstock, Inc.; page 14, ©privilege/Shutterstock, Inc.;
page 18, ©3445128471/Shutterstock, Inc.; page 21, ©iStockphoto.com/
merrymoonmary

Library of Congress Cataloging-in-Publication Data
Minden, Cecilia.
  How to write a letter/by Cecilia Minden and Kate Roth.
     p. cm.—(Language arts explorer junior)
  Includes bibliographical references and index.
  ISBN-13: 978-1-60279-991-2 (lib. bdg.)
  ISBN-10: 1-60279-991-1 (lib. bdg.)
  1. Letter writing—Juvenile literature. 2. English language—Composition
and exercises—Juvenile literature. I. Roth, Kate. II. Title.
  PE1483.M56 2011
  808.6—dc22   2010030062

Cherry Lake Publishing would like to acknowledge the work
of The Partnership for 21st Century Skills. Please visit
www.21stcenturyskills.org for more information.

Printed in the United States of America
Corporate Graphics Inc.
January 2011
CLSP08

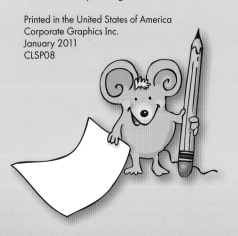

Table of Contents

CHAPTER ONE

A Friendly Letter

Receiving a letter from a friend is fun.

Did you ever get a letter in the mail? It is fun to have someone send a letter just to you. You can write a **friendly letter**, too. Think how happy a friend or loved one would be to get a letter from you. Let's get started!

A friendly letter has five main parts:

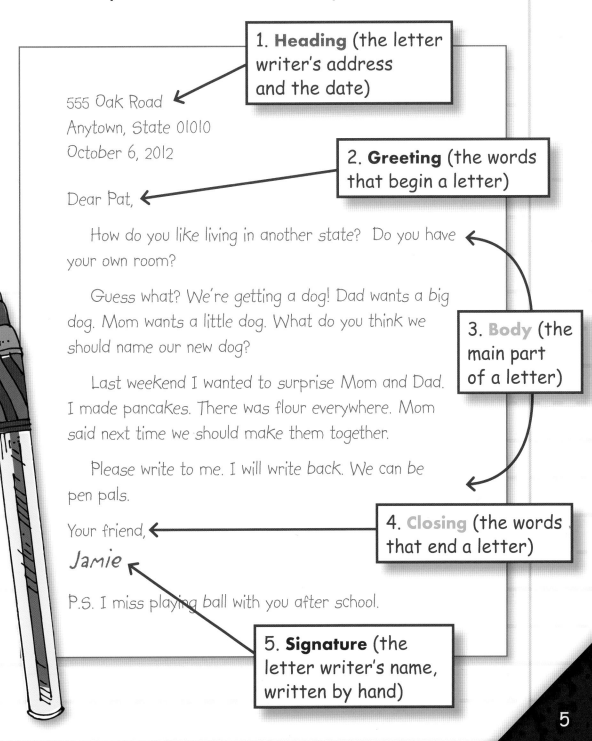

1. **Heading** (the letter writer's address and the date)

555 Oak Road
Anytown, State 01010
October 6, 2012

2. **Greeting** (the words that begin a letter)

Dear Pat,

How do you like living in another state? Do you have your own room?

Guess what? We're getting a dog! Dad wants a big dog. Mom wants a little dog. What do you think we should name our new dog?

Last weekend I wanted to surprise Mom and Dad. I made pancakes. There was flour everywhere. Mom said next time we should make them together.

Please write to me. I will write back. We can be pen pals.

3. **Body** (the main part of a letter)

Your friend,

4. **Closing** (the words that end a letter)

Jamie

P.S. I miss playing ball with you after school.

5. **Signature** (the letter writer's name, written by hand)

Stationery comes in many colors.

Stationery is special paper. It is used for writing letters. Sometimes, it comes with matching **envelopes**. You could also use plain paper and white envelopes.

Here's what you'll need to complete the activities in this book:

- Clean notebook paper
- Stationery and envelope
- Stamp
- Pencil with an eraser
- Pen
- **Dictionary**

Collect what you need.

CHAPTER TWO

Greetings!

Start by choosing a pen pal.

Who will get your letter? This helps you decide what you will write. Maybe your grandpa lives far away. You want him to be your pen pal. This is someone who writes to you and you write back to him.

Grab a pencil and a sheet of paper. Let's start writing a friendly letter!

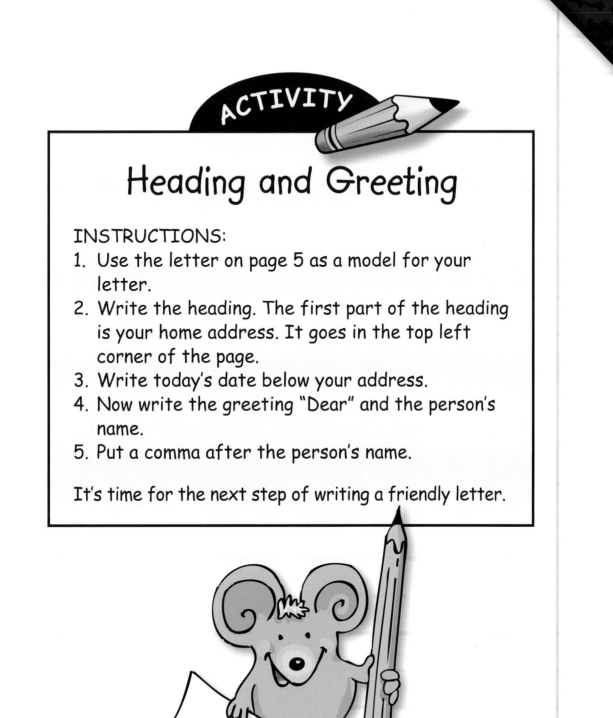

Heading and Greeting

INSTRUCTIONS:

1. Use the letter on page 5 as a model for your letter.
2. Write the heading. The first part of the heading is your home address. It goes in the top left corner of the page.
3. Write today's date below your address.
4. Now write the greeting "Dear" and the person's name.
5. Put a comma after the person's name.

It's time for the next step of writing a friendly letter.

CHAPTER THREE

Read All About It!

Your news goes in the body of the letter. What news would you like to share? What would the person you are writing to enjoy reading?

You can write about your family's trip to the zoo.

Make a short list of ideas for your letter. Here are some examples:

- a book you enjoyed reading
- a family trip to the zoo
- funny tricks you taught your pet
- how you played on a sports team

Maybe you can send a photo of your pet along with your letter.

Body

INSTRUCTIONS:

1. Take out a separate sheet of notebook paper. Choose two ideas from your list. Write each idea on one line of the notebook paper. Leave space between the ideas.
2. Write two or three sentences about each idea. These sentences will become a **paragraph**.
3. You can also write questions. Your pen pal will answer the questions when he or she writes back.
4. Work on your sentences until they are just right. Use a dictionary to check your spelling.
5. Use the letter you started earlier. Use a pen to copy your paragraphs to the letter.
6. **Indent** each paragraph. Look at the letter on page 5 to see indented paragraphs.

Now you have the body of your friendly letter. What do you think comes next?

IDEAS FOR MY LETTER

1. THE ZOO:

Last week we went to the zoo. I like to look at the snakes. What is your favorite part of the zoo?

2. SOCCER TRYOUTS:

Tryouts for the soccer team are on Saturday. I have been practicing kicking the ball around with my friends at the park. I hope we all make the team.

CHAPTER FOUR

P.S. Sign Your Name!

Some people like to think up funny closings for their letters.

The closing is how you say good-bye. There are many different closings. Choose one you like.

Write your signature below the closing. Sign only your first name if you know the person well.

Did you forget something? Add a postscript, or P.S. This is a short message that goes below your name.

Closing and Signature

INSTRUCTIONS:
1. Choose a closing for your letter. Here are some examples:
   - Your friend,
   - Laughs and lollipops,
   - Yours truly,
2. Make sure the first letter of the first word is uppercase. The rest of the words should be lowercase.
3. Put a comma at the end of the closing.
4. Sign your name below the closing.
5. If needed, add a P.S. below your signed name.

Miss you,

Your closing can reflect how you feel.

The Envelope, Please

Your letter is finished! All that is left is to put it in an envelope. There are post offices all over the world. They take care of a lot of mail. Help them by making sure everything on the envelope is correct.

Don't forget the stamp!

Jaime Johnson
555 Oak Road
Anytown, State 01010

USA FIRST-CLASS FOREVER

Grandpa Johnson
123 State Street
Anytown, State 01010

ACTIVITY

Addressing an Envelope

INSTRUCTIONS:
1. The **seal flap** should be at the top.
2. Be sure to write on the front of the envelope.
3. Write your name and address in the upper left corner.
4. Write the name and address of the person getting the letter in the center of the envelope.
5. Put a stamp in the upper right corner.

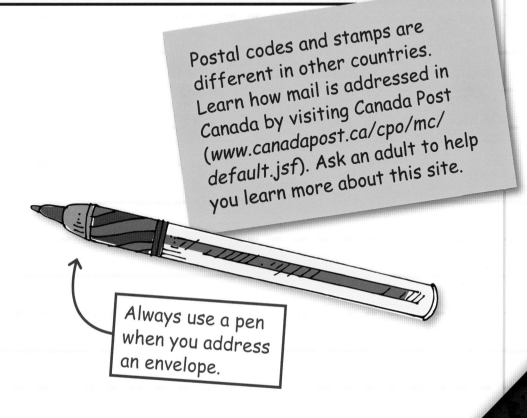

Postal codes and stamps are different in other countries. Learn how mail is addressed in Canada by visiting Canada Post (*www.canadapost.ca/cpo/mc/default.jsf*). Ask an adult to help you learn more about this site.

Always use a pen when you address an envelope.

CHAPTER SIX

Ready to Mail

It is almost time to mail your letter!

Check everything one more time:

☐ YES ☐ NO 1. Did I write a heading in the upper left corner?

☐ YES ☐ NO 2. Did I use the greeting "Dear"?

☐ YES ☐ NO 3. Did I spell the person's name correctly?

STOP! DON'T WRITE IN THE BOOK!

☐ YES ☐ NO 4. Did I remember a comma after the name?

☐ YES ☐ NO 5. Is the body of the letter clear and easy to understand?

☐ YES ☐ NO 6. Are my paragraphs indented?

☐ YES ☐ NO 7. Did I spell all words correctly?

☐ YES ☐ NO 8. Did I include a closing?

☐ YES ☐ NO 9. If the closing is more than one word, does only the first word begin with a capital letter?

☐ YES ☐ NO 10. Did I remember the comma?

☐ YES ☐ NO 11. Did I sign my name?

☐ YES ☐ NO 12. Does the envelope have my address and the reader's address?

☐ YES ☐ NO 13. Is there a stamp in the top right corner?

Did you answer yes to all of the questions? Good job!

555 Oak Road
Anytown, State 01010
October 6, 2012

Dear Grandpa,

How do you like living in your new house? Do you have a garden where you can grow vegetables?

Last week we went to the zoo. I like to look at the snakes. What is your favorite part of the zoo?

Tryouts for the soccer team are on Saturday. My friends and I have been practicing kicking the ball at the park. I hope we all make the team!

Please write me back, Grandpa. We can be pen pals.

Love and lollipops,

Jamie

P.S. When are you coming to visit us? I miss you!

Can you name all of the parts of this letter?

Your friends and family members will be happy when your letter arrives!

Now, put your letter in the envelope. Seal it shut. Don't forget to mail the letter! It won't take too long to reach the reader. Soon, you may find a letter in the mail just for you!

Glossary

body (BOD-ee) the main part of a letter

closing (KLOH-zing) the ending of a letter

dictionary (DIK-shuh-ner-ee) a book that lists words and their meanings

envelopes (ON-vuh-lohpss) flat paper coverings that are used to mail letters

greeting (GREE-ting) the opening words of a letter, such as *Dear Sally,*

friendly letter (FREND-lee LET-ur) a letter written to someone you know, such as a friend or family member

heading (HED-ing) the writer's address and the date, written at the top of a letter

indent (in-DENT) to start a line of writing farther in from the left edge of a page than the other lines

paragraph (PAIR-uh-graf) a group of sentences about a certain idea or subject

postscript (POHST-skript) a message that begins with "P.S." and is added to a letter below the writer's signed name

seal flap (SEEL FLAP) the part of an envelope that folds down to close it

signature (SIG-nuh-chur) a person's name signed by hand

stationery (STAY-shuh-ner-ee) special paper used for letter writing

For More Information

BOOKS

Jarnow, Jill. *Writing to Correspond*. New York: PowerKids Press, 2006.

Loewen, Nancy. *Sincerely Yours: Writing Your Own Letter*. Minneapolis: Picture Window Books, 2009.

WEB SITES

KidsHealth—Five Steps to Better Handwriting
kidshealth.org/kid/grow/school_stuff/handwriting.html
Neatness counts when writing letters! Find tips for better handwriting here.

PBS Kids—Letter
pbskids.org/arthur/games/letterwriter/letter.html
Look here to learn more about the parts of a letter.

Index

About the Authors

Cecilia Minden, PhD, is the former Director of the Language and Literacy Program at Harvard Graduate School of Education. While at Harvard, Dr. Minden taught several writing courses for teachers. She is now a full-time literacy consultant and the author of more than 100 books for children. Dr. Minden lives in Chapel Hill, North Carolina, with her husband, Dave Cupp, and a cute but spoiled Yorkie named Kenzie.

Kate Roth has a Doctorate from Harvard University in Language and Literacy and a Masters from Columbia University Teachers College in Curriculum and Teaching. Her work focuses on writing instruction in the primary grades. She has taught first grade, kindergarten, and Reading Recovery. She has also instructed hundreds of teachers from around the world in early literacy practices. She lives in Shanghai, China, with her husband and three children, ages 2, 6, and 9. They do a lot of writing to stay in touch with friends and family and to record their experiences.